Happy Easter Chad
Love, Kevin & Jan

FINDING *Hope*

{ *Where to Look for God's Help*

S. MICHAEL WILCOX

DESERET
BOOK

SALT LAKE CITY, UTAH

Library of Congress Cataloging-in-Publication Data

Wilcox, S. Michael, author.
    Finding hope : where to look for God's help / S. Michael Wilcox.
        pages cm — (A time out classic)
    ISBN 978-1-60908-067-9 (hardbound : alk. paper)
    1. Hope—Religious aspects—Church of Jesus Christ of Latter-day Saints.   2. Christian life—Mormon authors.   I. Title.   II. Series: Time out classics.
    BX8643.H67W54 2011
    234'.25—dc23   2011019749

Printed in Mexico
R. R. Donnelley, Reynosa, Mexico

10   9   8   7   6   5   4   3   2   1

IN THE VALLEY
OF DRY BONES

*G*od spoke to the great prophets of the Old Testament in some rather unique ways, most of them deeply visual. Ezekiel had wonderful visions that would grasp his hearers' imagination, causing them to pay attention and think profoundly. In one of those visions he saw a great valley of dry bones bleaching in the sun. Visualize that scene with me for just a moment. Before us is a wide valley, filled with bones as far as the eye can see in every direction. A great army or a mighty people have all died, and their bones lie exposed to the weather. Ezekiel stands "in the midst of the valley," when the Lord enters the scene and causes Ezekiel "to pass by [the bones] round about . . .

and, lo, they were very dry" (Ezekiel 37:1–2). After Ezekiel makes a circuit of the valley, the Lord addresses His prophet with a question: "Son of man, can these bones live?"

Ezekiel responds in a purely human way: "O Lord God, thou knowest" (Ezekiel 37:3). In other words, "Why are you asking me?"

The Lord then continues, "Prophesy upon these bones, and say unto them, O ye dry bones, . . . I will cause breath to enter into you, and ye shall live" (Ezekiel 37:4–5). Ezekiel prophesies, and the Lord's words come true.

Ezekiel describes a quite dramatic moment, complete with sound. Now, along with our visualization, we need to listen and we'll hear "a noise, and behold a shaking, and the bones came together, bone to his bone" (Ezekiel 37:7). We can visualize this; we can hear it—all those bones rattling and clacking together, the ribs lining up, the skulls reattaching. We see this great army of skeletons gathered there, but they need the clothing of flesh. While Ezekiel watches, "Lo, the sinews and the flesh came up upon them, and the skin covered them above" (Ezekiel

37:8). But there is still no life in them. They're just assembled there, waiting.

With that unbelievable question still fresh in our minds, "Can these bones live?" the Lord tells Ezekiel to prophesy again: "Prophesy unto the wind, prophesy, son of man, and say to the wind, Thus saith the Lord God; Come from the four winds, O breath, and breathe upon these slain, that they may live" (Ezekiel 37:9). And Ezekiel prophesies! Ezekiel calls the four winds. Let us see this moment in our imagination. The winds sweep down from the four cardinal points of the compass and pass through the lifeless men. Then—you can hear it—that great army draws in breath and lives, "and [stands] up upon their feet, an exceeding great army" (Ezekiel 37:10).

What is the purpose of this remarkable vision? Is it a witness of the Resurrection? Perhaps the Lord has something else in mind. He teaches Ezekiel what his wonderful vision of the dry bones was about. It has a powerful meaning, necessary for all of our lives. The Lord says, "Son of man, these bones are the whole house of Israel: behold, they say, Our bones are dried, and *our hope is lost"* (Ezekiel 37:11; emphasis added).

The Lord desires for us to realize, through that powerful vision Ezekiel experienced, that though our hopes may be dead and dried and bleaching in the sun, we are to anticipate the breath of God. Then there will be a great noise and a shaking, and our hopes will come together again, stand up, and draw in breath. We will know that moment in our own lives when the great army stands and steps forward boldly into the future.

Let us explore some of what the Lord gives us in the scriptures so that we can have that moment of drawing in breath, then watching as our hopes rise into life. Much of this depends on us. It will happen if we only know where to look. Hope is a creation as well as a gift!

No Hope in
the Dictionary

When I was notified of the 2010 Time Out for Women theme, "Infinite Hope," it reminded me of an experience I had many years ago. I was preparing a talk on faith, hope, and charity. I decided I would start in the Bible Dictionary and see what I could find there. I searched for those three words alphabetically. I started with charity, looking up what the Bible Dictionary said about charity, and collected some scriptures on that theme. I found much that was helpful.

Then it was on to faith. I found good information and references about faith, which I searched and consequently harvested some wonderful ideas. Last, I turned to hope. What do you think I discovered? It wasn't there! *Hope* is not in the Bible Dictionary. I was amazed! Just to make sure it wasn't only my Bible Dictionary, I asked a friend, "Would you please check your Bible and see if *hope* is in the Bible Dictionary?" It wasn't in hers, either. I had to work a little to find stories and verses about hope around which I could construct my talk.

Perhaps this little experience is indicative of our lives. We have to *look* for hope! We have to create it! I went on a journey through the scriptures to find hope. I would like to share some of the stories that surfaced. They have helped me when my hopes are like lifeless bones drying in a wide valley, devoid of the breath of God.

WALLS AND GIANTS OR
MILK AND HONEY

*M*ost often what you find hinges on where you look. Hope shines in many different directions. The first scripture story deals with finding hope by looking forward. In a forward focus we usually find renewed optimism. Yet even here we must choose what to see in the future. One of my favorite Old Testament stories is in the book of Numbers. When Moses and the children of Israel were preparing to enter the promised land, they sent twelve spies ahead into Canaan, a leader from each of the tribes, to search the land and report on what they saw. The spies traveled throughout Canaan for forty days, assessing, observing, and gathering information. When those twelve men came back, two different reports were given.

Joshua and Caleb, the two spies representing Ephraim and Judah, gave their report to the listening people, along with a visual aid. "They came unto the brook of Eshcol, and cut down from thence a branch with one cluster of grapes, and they bare it between two upon a staff; and they brought of the pomegranates, and of the figs" (Numbers 13:23). They described the land with a phrase that is now proverbial: "And surely it floweth with milk and honey; and this is the fruit of it" (Numbers 13:27). There, for all of Israel to see, hangs a large cluster of grapes. (In fact, the symbol of Israel's tourist industry today is a depiction of Joshua and Caleb carrying a huge bunch of grapes on a pole between them.) These two spies saw the fruits of the land: the grapes and the pomegranates and the figs. It was the milk and honey they were focused on. Within that focus, hope, desire, and courage were born.

The report from the other spies was not as rosy: "Nevertheless the people be strong that dwell in the land, and the cities are walled, and very great. . . .

We be not able to go up against the people; for they are stronger than we. . . . And there we saw the giants, the sons of Anak . . . and we were in our own sight as grasshoppers, and so we were in their sight" (Numbers 13:28, 31, 33). That is quite a different report. Yet, if we think about it, both reports were essentially true. It is not the case that one was correct and the other incorrect. Each was a reliable statement of the facts. The point that this story makes, however, is that we need to look beyond the walls and the giants to the grapes and the pomegranates. We need to look to the milk and honey that we can see if we look farther forward.

Frequently in life we need to move forward with hope in spite of all the distractions and obstacles, even when we perceive that they are "stronger than we." I work with young people a great deal and have observed that, at times, they need hope to move forward in their schooling or in forming an eternal marriage. We may face giants and walls in financial concerns, in the development and growth of a child, in employment, in mastering a talent or skill. The list can be extensive, but the principle remains constant in all areas. Whatever challenge we may face as parents, as spouses, in callings, with trials, even at the death of a loved one, we need to move forward by looking forward. As we look forward, we have a choice of what we can focus on. We can gaze on the fruits that are ahead. We can see the grapes and the figs and the pomegranates, the rewards, joys, and fulfillments that are awaiting us. Or we can see the walls keeping us from them. We can stare at the giants, and, in our own sight, appear as grasshoppers in facing those great challenges. But if we will learn to look at the fruits that await us, not the barriers, not the walls—there will always be walls, and giants to fight—our courage and hope will be enlivened. We will be assured that the fruits on the other side are worth it.

THE WALLS CAME TUMBLING DOWN

*W*hen I was little my aunt sent me at times to pick currants and gooseberries that grew wild in the canyon. When I returned, she would make gooseberry or currant jam. Fresh jam meant we could have flapjacks. There were enormous stacks of flapjacks smothered with homemade jam. It was a fantastic treat! However, there were thorns on those berry bushes, and occasionally when I was picking currants and gooseberries—and they are very small berries; she needed a lot of them for jam—a voice inside my head would say, "You can live without the flapjacks and jam, without the fruits. It's not that important." This argument was always countered by another, and seconded by my taste buds, which said, "You can bear with a few pricked fingers." When we need hope, it is important that we always look forward to the fruits. Pricked fingers will heal.

In another book of the Bible, we encounter the wonderful ending to the story of Joshua and Caleb, which takes place many years later than their spy mission to Canaan. The first generation of the Exodus, panicked by the giants and by the walls, ended up wandering forty years in the wilderness. This episode with the walls and the giants was the last straw. The Lord knew He couldn't bring that generation into the promised land. Joshua and Caleb would be allowed entry, but the other spies— and their frightened listeners—forfeited the opportunity. So Israel wandered for forty years, until the next generation had been schooled in the wilderness and had developed a firmer faith. If we don't see the hope by looking forward, past the walls and the giants, we can end up wandering, distracted, our lives out of focus. We may miss wonderful opportunities which would be very desirable.

Continuing our story, we look at what happened

to the next generation, the wilderness generation, those who learned to follow Joshua and Caleb's leadership. As the Israelites crossed the Jordan River into their new homeland, the first city they encountered was Jericho. We all know the story of Jericho. The dominant aspect of that story concerns the walls of Jericho. We can sing the chorus of the old spiritual, "And the walls came a-tumbling down." This is the last chapter of the story of the spies. We will miss a relevant lesson if we do not connect the two encounters. When we look for the fruits and make them our focus, we receive help from higher sources, and the walls that formerly held us back ultimately come down. We can count on this. It is sad that Israel had to wait forty years to discover this truth.

CAMPING ON
THE BEACH

There is another story, in the Book of Mormon this time, that can enhance the message of the story of the twelve spies. As the Jaredites moved forward toward their promised land, they had to build barges and boats to cross smaller bodies of water. Eventually they came to the ocean, the ultimate crossing. Before we examine what they did at this point in their journey, I would like to point out that all of the major journeys and almost all crossings in the scriptures —be they deserts, wilderness, oceans, or the Jordan River— should be read with our own lives in mind. We too are making a journey to the eternal promised land, the celestial kingdom. There will be critical crossings during that journey, moments when decisions are made which will change our lives forever. There can be no turning back. Crossings must be made with courage, hope, and faith. We must apply to our own progress all the lessons, challenges, and hopes in the biblical or Book of Mormon stories. They will clarify life for us in a magnificent manner.

Before the Jaredites reached their greatest barrier, crossing the ocean, the Lord made an important comment that is easy to miss; yet it is critical that we apply it to our own journey so that we may receive our eternal reward. It is true of the Lord's hopes for us also.

"And the Lord would not suffer that they should stop beyond the sea in the wilderness [a smaller crossing], but he would that they should come forth even unto the land of promise, which was choice above all other lands" (Ether 2:7). It is the same with us! The Lord does not wish us to engage in half a journey. He wants us to make the whole journey, and not let great barriers that seem to bar our way forward, or that we perceive to be beyond our ability to advance past, to stop us. He desires the whole journey because He desires us to reach the final destination. We must not be satisfied with less than the promised land that is choice above all other lands.

When the Jaredites arrived at the ocean, they camped on the beach for four years. That's quite a beach party. Four years! The brother of Jared, who is a faithful and a praying man, didn't seem to do anything for four years. They just sat on the beach. I have often wondered about those four years. Why didn't the brother of Jared find a way forward?

There may be two reasons why they sat on the beach. Both are instructive when we find ourselves facing an ocean and the sand is warm underfoot and soft breezes blow.

First, perhaps they had reached a comfort level which was hard to break out of because they were satisfied with where they were.

"Sure, the promised land would be great. We'll get there someday, but right now life is good."

They were happy with the beach. They didn't progress in their journey because they were contented and secure. There are times when I reach a plateau or a level where I am comfortable, reasonably happy, at ease with myself, and I don't move forward. I hope you understand that feeling. I'd hate to be baring my soul alone, everyone else thinking, "I haven't the slightest idea what he means. I'm always pressing forward steadfastly. Nephi and I must have been cut out of the same mold."

Second, perhaps the Jaredites sat for four years on the beach because their obstacle was so massive. They had success crossing the smaller seas or lakes, but the ocean . . . that was another thing altogether. How in the world could something so enormous be crossed? So they just sat. Perhaps the brother of Jared waited for the Lord to tell him what to do while he camped. We can reasonably conclude from his portrayal in Ether that the brother of Jared did not have an overly aggressive personality. He always deferred to his brother Jared. Perhaps it was a matter of initiative, even one of inertia.

But finally the Lord came and chastened the brother of Jared "because he remembered not to call upon the name of the Lord" (Ether 2:14). We can always ask the Lord for counsel, strength, insight, wisdom—whatever is needed to continue with our journey. Now, I suppose He could give us the needed directions without being asked, but it seems that He likes being asked, especially after we have puzzled through the dilemma ourselves. The Jaredites might have anticipated they would be given instructions. After all, they were, up to this point, "being directed continually by the hand of the Lord" (Ether 2:6). Maybe they took it for granted that the directions would come and simply failed to exercise their own minds and souls in finding a solution to the great challenge they faced.

I can relate to all of these scenarios; I assume you can also. Let us anticipate that, when we stand gazing across those broad oceans in our lives, the Lord will instruct us on how to build the right kind of barge to get across it. So let's ask.

MOVING
MOUNTAINS

used to be very troubled by a certain saying of our Savior. He taught that if we had faith no larger than a mustard seed we could move mountains. That verse caused me a lot of distress. It produced a certain amount of guilt. I knew I did not have that faith. I was reading that verse literally. We make big mistakes sometimes by our too-literal reading of scriptures that were meant to be understood on a figurative level. If we interpret this saying literally, then it is really a worthless verse, because it would have application to so few people over the entire history of the world. I do not believe that God deals in valueless truths. After all, how many people would need to actually move a mountain and, if the need actually arose, how many people would have that kind of faith?

If we examine it on the figurative level, it will feed all humanity. Rather than the literal meaning, the verse means that if we have even a little faith, we can overcome, climb over, or go around any obstacle—"the mountain," in the Savior's words— that stands in our way. A mustard seed is so very small, and a mountain so very large. That is just the point—it doesn't take a great amount of faith, in either the Lord or ourselves, to face the mountainous obstacles that hold us back. We can move them!

If we are willing to move forward, in spite of walls, giants, seas, or mountains, God will help us. We need to understand that, in our relationship with our Father in Heaven, levels of comfort or great obstacles are not an excuse to quit our journey. He intends on getting us there. If we will try to move forward, if we'll call upon Him for help in facing those obstacles, He will teach us how to build the barges, or tell us to keep marching around the walls until they come tumbling down. When you need hope, look forward, beyond the walls, beyond the giants, beyond the oceans, over the mountains to the promised land—to the fruits, to the pomegranates, to the figs, to the joys. And you will create in your own hearts the hope necessary to progress.

BEARS AND LIONS

*S*ometimes, when we need hope, we must look backward. In looking backward we will find moments in our past experiences that will generate hope. There will be something that has happened to us, something that God has placed in our own lives previously, that is designed specifically for a future challenge. Or His wisdom will find and bring into our minds experiences we have gained which are exactly what we need at the present moment. One of the greatest stories in the Bible that illustrates this truth is the story of David facing Goliath. We all face Goliaths in our lives. But remember that the children of Israel were afraid of the giants. In this story, we have one, and he is fully armed and threatening. Perhaps the assessment of the ten spies was correct after all. No one was willing to meet the Philistine, including Saul, who we are told, "from his shoulders and upward he was higher than any of the people" (1 Samuel 9:2). Saul was the obvious choice to face the giant in battle, but he too was afraid.

David had something in his past, however, that told him he could meet Goliath. Notice what he said that convinced Saul to put all Israel's fate into (in Saul's eyes) an untested youth's hands. Where did David obtain the hope and assurance to walk alone down the hill and into the broad valley of Elah to meet the vastly more powerful Goliath?

"Thy servant kept his father's sheep, and there came a lion, and a bear, and took a lamb out of the flock: and I went out after him, and smote him, and delivered it out of his mouth. . . . Thy servant slew both the lion and the bear: and this uncircumcised Philistine shall be as one of them. . . . The Lord that delivered me out of the paw of the lion, and out of the paw of the bear, he will deliver me out of the hand of this Philistine" (1 Samuel 17:34–37).

In David's past, there had been smaller challenges. We can liken this, in some degree, to the Jaredites building less-seaworthy barges to cross the inland seas. In our lives also there will be smaller challenges, lion and bear moments. I sometimes wonder if David thought, when the lion and then the bear charged at him, that he was one unlucky shepherd. I wonder if he prayed to the Lord and said, "Lord, what did I do to deserve a lion and a bear?" The Lord might have answered, "Because one day you will face a Goliath. The courage and the faith and the power and the hope that you will need to face that Goliath, that larger challenge, will have been created within you. You will have discovered in yourself the inner resources demanded, because you first faced the lion and the bear. I'm doing you a favor by sending lions and bears!" When you need hope, look back to the lion and the bear moments of your life when you developed those inner resources.

The Wrong Way
to Look Back

*O*ne of the great problems with the children of Israel during Moses' generation was their inability to look to the past miracles and protections the Lord had granted them. They did look back, but their looking back was second cousin to their looking forward at the ten spies' report. It didn't seem to matter how many times God brought water from the rock, or split the Red Sea, or humbled Pharaoh, or fed them with manna—it was never enough. All they saw looking backward was the easier life in Egypt, and Egypt's "fish, [and] the cucumbers, and the melons, and the leeks, and the onions, and the garlick" (Numbers 11:5). Never mind that *that* life had been one of bondage and toil. To the Israelites, it was at least a more secure life than following Moses through a barren wilderness.

Given the choice of freedom with faith or bondage with security, they could not get their eyes off the fleshpots of the past. Yet there were many other memories they could have turned to that would have created the needed hope. Ultimately, the Lord must ask Himself and Moses, "How long will this people provoke me? and how long will it be ere they believe me, for all the signs which I have shewed among them?" (Numbers 14:11).

"GOD HEARS"

*T*he Lord shows us this same way of looking backward for a source of hope in the story of Hagar. Hagar is an example for every mother raising a child by herself. There was a moment earlier in her life when God prepared Hagar for a greater challenge that arrived when she and her son found themselves alone and desperate in the desert near Beer-sheba in the south of Canaan.

Before Ishmael's birth, Hagar had wandered in that same desert, running from a confrontation with Sarah. An angel appeared to Hagar. She was in the wilderness, alone, and pregnant with Ishmael. The angel asked her two questions: "Whence camest thou? and whither wilt thou go?" (Genesis 16:8).

Do you ever find yourself in a similar position, asking yourself similar questions? "How did I get here? Where am I going to go? What am I going to do?" Sometimes we get ourselves into difficult situations; sometimes life creates them. The important thing is what we are going to do once we are in them.

The angel continued: "Behold, thou art with child, and shalt bear a son, and shalt call his name Ishmael; because the Lord hath heard thy affliction" (Genesis 16:11). Names in the Bible, in Genesis in particular, are critical. We need to know the Hebrew meaning of each name because often a story's theme is contained in the name or names of its principal characters. *Ishmael* means "God hears." God hears! That is the theme of Hagar's, and Ishmael's, story.

The Lord instructed Hagar to name her son "God hears." He knew that that name would be important later in Hagar's life and, in a broader context, for countless people throughout generations. Several years later, when Ishmael had grown to be a young teenage boy, Hagar found herself alone and in critically desperate straits. Here we learn the rest of the story and the importance of the name given to Ishmael in the past.

Sarah, fearing for her son Isaac, asked Abraham to separate him from Ishmael; the Lord confirmed her wisdom. "[Hagar] departed, and wandered in the wilderness of Beer-sheba. And the water was spent in the bottle, and she cast the child under one of the shrubs. And she went, and sat her down over against him a good way off, . . . for she said, Let me not see the death of the child. And she sat over against him, and lift up her voice, and wept" (Genesis 21:14–16).

Do we remember the name of the boy that was perishing in the shade under a shrub? Both he and his mother were on the verge of death. But what is the boy's name? He is called "God hears." The next words we read in Genesis, therefore, come naturally: "And *God heard* the voice of the lad; and the angel of God called to Hagar out of heaven, and said unto her, What aileth thee, Hagar? fear not; for *God hath heard* the voice of the lad where he is. Arise, lift up the lad, and hold him in thine hand. . . . And

God opened her eyes, and she saw a well of water" (Genesis 21:17–19; emphasis added).

That is a powerful story! It is particularly important for those of the Islamic faith, who trace their spiritual ancestry through Ishmael, not Isaac. Millions and millions of people reenact this story year after year in Mecca during the Hajj. The story of Hagar bears testimony that *God hears.* No matter who you are or what circumstances you may find yourself facing, God hears. But God planted that name, and that lesson contained in a name, in Hagar's son years before her moment of desperation, when she needed to know that her Father in Heaven was aware of her. When you need hope, look backward. There will be experiences in your past that will bring hope to fill the present need. Or perhaps the present need is the very experience you will look back to in a future time of urgency.

A Child's Prayer

*W*hen I was twelve years old, I was asked to give an opening prayer in stake conference. I was terrified. I was a brand-new deacon. It was a crowd of about 1,800 people, and I was a little deacon. I didn't begin to grow until I was sixteen or seventeen years old. Actually, when I was eighteen, my own grandmother asked me if I'd received the priesthood yet. That's how short I was. I was shorter than any of my friends. I had a nice growth spurt when I began eating French pastries in the mission field.

I can remember I could barely see over the top of the pulpit, and I offered a very simple child's prayer. I didn't think a thing about it until ten years later, when a woman in one of the other wards in that stake came up to me. I had just returned home from my mission.

She said, "Mike, I need to thank you. You changed my life."

I said, "I can't think of anything I've ever done for you."

"You won't remember this," she replied, "but when you were twelve years old you gave a prayer in stake conference. I was struggling in my life at that time. I didn't believe God heard my prayers anymore. But there was something about the image before me of a boy praying that reminded me of my own prayers as a little girl. As I thought of my prayers as a child, and how firmly I believed, all my faith came flooding back and I knew in my heart that God heard me and cared. I want to thank you."

I didn't change that woman's life. She was gracious to say so, but all I did was offer a prayer in a stake conference. Yet something in her past was awakened at that time. The hope that she needed came from her own experience, not from my prayer. When you need hope, look back.

Thinking of a little girl's prayers reminds me of

my own daughter, Megan. We bought her a pink toy telephone when she was a little girl. (Considering the time she spent on telephones in her subsequent life, I'm not sure that was a good decision.) She used to have wonderful long conversations with imaginary people on her pink phone. One day I came home from work and found her carrying on quite a serious conversation with someone. She was about four years old. She was so intense that I interrupted her and asked, "Megan, who are you talking to?"

She looked up at me, rather annoyed at the intrusion, and said, "It's Jesus!" She then turned back to her phone. I was intrigued, so I risked one more interruption.

"What is He saying to you, Megan?" I asked.

Once again, and with a little more irritation in her voice and face, she put the phone down and said, "He's telling me to get married in the temple!"

I almost picked up the phone myself at this point and said, "Hello?"

Megan established in her early childhood and youth the habit of a familiar relationship with her Father in Heaven, a pink telephone relationship. One day while she was hurrying downstairs she slipped on a stair and fell. Life has a way of combining circumstances at times to produce rather unpleasant results. As fate would have it, my wife had left a glass on the lower step and Megan fell on it, cutting her arm quite badly and severing a nerve. Surgery was done to repair the damage, but weeks of therapy awaited, with no major hope that the nerve would regenerate fast enough to prevent the muscles in her hand from atrophying and causing permanent damage.

I was as worried about my wife as I was my daughter because my wife blamed herself for leaving the glass on the stairs. I could see her carrying a load of mother-guilt throughout her life. We all prayed fervently that the nerve would grow in time and looked to the medical community for encouragement. One morning, Megan walked upstairs and said, "We don't have to worry about my arm. I prayed and Heavenly Father told me it would be all right." She was so matter-of-fact about her announcement. My wife and I had turned to doctors, therapy, and surgery for hope. Megan picked up her "pink telephone" and talked to her Father.

The Road
to Emmaus

*W*hen you need hope, look beside you. One of my favorite stories in the life of Christ is the journey He took with two disciples on the road to Emmaus immediately after the Resurrection. Put yourself in that journey. Wherever you are in your life, you are on the road to your own Emmaus. Allow the words of this afternoon walk on the day of Christ's Resurrection to create the hope necessary for you.

"And, behold, two of them went that same day to a village called Emmaus. . . . And they talked together of all these things which had happened. And it came to pass, that, while they communed together and reasoned, Jesus himself drew near, and went with them. But their eyes were holden that they should not know him. And he said unto them, What manner of communications are these that ye have one to another, as ye walk, and are sad? And the one of them . . . said unto him, Art thou only a stranger in Jerusalem, and hast not known the things which are come to pass there in these days?'" (Luke 24:13–18).

Are there times in your life, the hope-searching times, when you say similar words? There are moments in my life when I say, "Lord, art thou only a stranger to me and my circumstances, and don't know what's happened?" Where is God? Is He aware?

Jesus responded to their amazement: "And he said unto them, What things?" (Luke 24:19). He invited them to tell Him their sorrows, to pour out their confusion and despair. And they did pour it out to Him as they walked, without knowing who the stranger was. We are invited to do the same thing.

They finally arrived at Emmaus; by this time they sensed something in this man who had walked calmly beside them with so much wisdom and solace. Their eyes were still "holden," but there was something remarkable and peaceful about this stranger. They said, "Abide with us." In two of our favorite hymns of peace, we sing, "Abide with me" (*Hymns*, nos. 165, 166).

We read these beautiful words, "And he went in to tarry with them" (Luke 24:29). We worship a "tarrying" Savior. Do you remember when in 3 Nephi the people, without speaking, wanted Him "to tarry a little longer with them"? (3 Nephi 17:5). He did!

Jesus broke bread with the two disciples. During that sacred moment, their eyes were finally opened. They recognized who the stranger was who spent the day with them, teaching and comforting them. "And they said one to another, Did not our heart burn within us, while he talked with us by the way, and while he opened to us the scriptures?" (Luke 24:32). There are times when He walks with us, and we're not aware, our eyes are holden, but we feel His influence and His love. Look beside you!

T. S. Eliot wrote a powerful poem entitled "The Waste Land." I read and studied it in high school and in college. Its title indicates something of the poem's outlook on life. Life can, from time to time, seem like a waste land where there is little beauty and not much lives. However, there is some hope in the poem. Eliot alluded to the story of the road to Emmaus to project that hope. I have quoted these lines to myself more times than I can relate. They are very beautiful. I offer them here to, I hope, light your own soul as they have lit mine:

> *Who is the third who walks always beside you?*
> *When I count, there are only you and I together*
> *But when I look ahead up the white road*
> *There is always another one walking beside you*
> *Gliding wrapt in a brown mantle, hooded*
> *I do not know whether a man or a woman*
> *—But who is that on the other side of you?*

(T. S. Eliot, "The Waste Land,"
in *The Waste Land and Other Writings*
[New York: Modern Library, 2002], 49)

WE WERE FOUR

I recently returned from a trip to Antarctica. I always wanted to travel to all seven continents. Now I've finally accomplished my goal. There is a wonderful story about an Antarctic explorer named Sir Ernest Shackleton, who made one of the most incredible journeys in exploration history. In brief, Shackleton and his men became icebound in their ship, the *Endurance,* in the Weddell Sea. It was a frozen prison which lasted for months, including the Antarctic winter, when the sun does not rise for months. During this time they floated in a circular motion towards the Antarctic Peninsula until the ice finally crushed the ship. They spent another period of months on large ice floes, stranded over thousands of feet of ocean water. As the ice floes melted and they reached open water, the crew abandoned the ice for three small lifeboats, spending days in freezing, harrowing conditions until they landed on an isolated outcropping of land named Elephant Island.

During their ordeal they lived off stores from the abandoned ship as well as seal and penguin meat. Because Elephant Island is far from the route of the seal and whaling ships, Shackleton knew that he couldn't expect rescue from a passing ship. So, in the most incredible open-boat journey I know of in man's history, in a 22-foot boat covered with a makeshift canvas top, he and five other men went for help across 850 miles of the most treacherous seas on the planet, known as the Drake Passage. They were trying to reach a tiny pinpoint of land named South George Island, where they could obtain help.

After days of battling storms, ice, and a towering rogue wave they miraculously found that small point of land. Unfortunately, they landed on the wrong side of the island from the whaling station and the help they needed. Their boat was no longer seaworthy. Three of them were so weak they could hardly walk. Shackleton and two others made a crossing over the glaciers and high mountains of South Georgia—thirty-six hours of incredible endurance—to drop into a whaling station on the other side. Shackleton was determined he would not lose a man of the twenty-eight men who trusted his leadership. And he succeeded!

Why recount that story? After Shackleton made that unbelievable final climb over the wilderness of South Georgia, Frank Worsley, his close friend and one of the other two men with him, made an interesting observation. Here is the account in Shackleton's own words:

"When I look back at those days I have no doubt that Providence guided us, not only across those snow fields, but across the storm-white sea that separated Elephant Island from our landing place on South Georgia. I know that during that long and racking march of thirty-six hours over the unnamed mountains and glaciers of South Georgia it seemed to me often that we were four, not three.

I said nothing to my companions on the point, but afterwards Worsley said to me, 'Boss, I had a curious feeling on the march that there was another person with us.' Crean confessed to the same idea. One feels 'the dearth of human words, the roughness of mortal speech' in trying to describe things intangible, but a record of our journeys would be incomplete without a reference to a subject very near to our hearts" (Sir Ernest Shackleton, *South: The Endurance Expedition* [New York: Penguin Classics, 2002], 204). They were four!

There will be times that, if we will look beside us, we will realize we are "four." That third man who walked with the disciples on the road to Emmaus will walk with us. Let us look beside us to find hope.

From Galaxies
to Children

*W*e can find hope in almost every place we look, especially if we look toward our God. Consider this wonderful scripture: "All things are created and made to bear record of me, . . . things which are in the heavens above, and things which are on the earth, . . . both above and beneath: all things bear record of me" (Moses 6:63).

Let me try to show you the arc that God's compass circumscribes. I'm sure most of you have seen the little nesting dolls that are associated with Russia and other Slavic countries. There are smaller and smaller dolls inside until they reach the size of a grain of rice. Each is individually painted. I have a set at home of thirty dolls, and the largest is barely the size of a small cantaloupe. By taking a short scriptural journey, we can compare the arc that God's concerns encompasses with our Russian nesting dolls. We will open the dolls one by one and attach a scripture to each opening. Pay close attention to particular words that are used as we narrow the reach in each verse of scripture.

The first truth we want to examine, the outside doll, is the greatest extent of God's kingdom. "Worlds without number have I created; . . . and innumerable are they unto man; but all things are *numbered* unto me, for they are mine and I *know* them" (Moses 1:33, 35; emphasis added). That arc is indeed a broad span. We can take the first outside doll as representative of "worlds without number." Notice the verbs *are numbered* and *know,* and also the phrase *they are mine.* The Lord affirms to His children that He numbers all His worlds, they are His, and He knows them.

Let us remove the outside doll and see what is inside. What is smaller than a world? A nation! On the title page of the Book of Mormon, the Lord tells us the purpose of the book. When we talk about the purpose of the Book of Mormon we usually discuss only half of one purpose. There are three that are mentioned. One purpose is to show us the "great things the Lord hath done for [our] fathers," inferring He will do the same for us, and another is to help us "know the covenants of the Lord." These two precede the one we always quote, but notice the crowning purpose, which is "the convincing of the Jew and Gentile that JESUS is the CHRIST, the ETERNAL GOD, *manifesting* himself unto all nations" (Book of Mormon title page; emphasis added).

The goal of the Book of Mormon is not only to convince the world that Jesus is the Christ, but to convince them that He will manifest Himself to all nations, or peoples. The key verb here is *manifesting*. The Lord tells us that He numbers all His worlds, He knows them, and He manifests Himself to every nation.

Let us open another layer and see what we can find. What is smaller than a nation? When the four sons of Mosiah came back from their fourteen-year mission among the Lamanites, they had learned a number of valuable lessons, which they shared with their people and with us. Ammon's conclusion, given in his homecoming address, was: "Blessed is the name of my God, who has been *mindful* of this people. . . ; yea, I say, blessed be the name of my God, who has been *mindful* of us, wanderers in a strange land. Now my brethren, we see that God is *mindful* of every people, whatsoever land they may be in; yea, he *numbereth* his people, and his bowels of mercy are over all the earth" (Alma 26:36–37; emphasis added). Our key word this time is *mindful*—Ammon used it three times. He also repeated the verb used in Moses, that of *numbered.* God numbers all His worlds and knows them. He manifests Himself to every nation. He is mindful of every people.

What is smaller than a people? We look deeper into the layers of God's concerns. We open another nesting doll. Therein we find a single person: one individual, one personality. If I were to pick the verse in the Book of Mormon that announces its witness better than anything else, I would pick the words of Alma the Younger as he emerged from the coma, or sleep, during which he had been forgiven of his sins and discovered the mercy of God and

Christ. Upon awakening, Alma addressed the waiting people and said, "I rejected my Redeemer, and denied that which had been spoken of by our fathers; but now that they may foresee that he will come, and that he *remembereth* every creature of his creating, he will make himself *manifest* unto all" (Mosiah 27:30; emphasis added).

We have here a new verb that shows the Lord's action, and another we have seen before is repeated—*remembereth* and *manifest.* God remembers every creature of His creating! Our Father in Heaven affirms that He numbers all His worlds and knows them. He manifests Himself to every nation. He is mindful of every people. He remembers every person. In response to the Savior's goodness, Alma testified that "every knee shall bow, and every tongue confess before him" (Mosiah 27:31).

Can we go smaller than a person? Open another layer and see what is inside. What is smaller than a person? A little person, a child. I know that bends the rules a little bit, but let us see what we can find in the scriptures about a child. In 3 Nephi, in those wonderful moments when Jesus has finished teaching the multitude and is about to depart, yet feels their desire that He remain, He asks for all the little children—the Junior Primary—to gather around Him. Then, groaning in Himself, He prays for them. His prayer is so beautiful it can't be recorded. Yet Jesus is not satisfied with a prayer for the children in general. This is not sufficient to express His love, so we read these words, "And when he had said these words, he wept, and the multitude bare record of it, and he took their little children, *one by one*, and *blessed* them, *and prayed* unto the Father for them" (3 Nephi 17:21; emphasis added). *One by one* is a beautiful and revealing phrase. So also are the verbs *to bless* and *to pray for*. Every child was blessed and prayed for individually by the Master. We are told there were 2,500 people in the multitude. We are not told how many were little children, but even a fraction would be a considerable number.

We look at our accumulation of expressions and together they present a powerful emotive effect. God numbers all His worlds and knows them. He manifests Himself to every nation. He is mindful of every people. He remembers every person. He blesses and prays for every child.

We could go on to the level of sparrows and the hairs on one's head, but we will stop here. It almost seems to me, as I read the Book of Mormon, that story after story is related to prove the point we have been making above. Think of the following people and events and the things that are said to them or that they say themselves. We have Enos, King Benjamin's people, Zeezrom, Alma the Younger and the sons of Mosiah, Lamoni, his father—the list goes on and on. They all receive the Savior's love and forgiveness and they receive it immediately upon asking. They are all people of whom the Lord was mindful, and to whom He manifested Himself in mercy and forgiveness. After all, they were His sheep and He had numbered them.

A Jewel from the
Savior's Crown

*A*s we look around us, from the largest galaxy to the smallest child, our eyes will eventually rest on one another. When we need hope we can always find it in each other's eyes and gifts.

A number of years ago I had a wonderful dream. In most of my dreams I am frantically trying to find a class at school and I can't remember where it is, my books are in my locker, and I can't remember my combination. Or I am moving in terribly slow motion, running from something or toward something and making no progress whatsoever. Do you have those sorts of dreams? I call them school nightmares. But this was a lovely dream. The kind sent to us by God, not drawn from our own subconscious fears and aspirations.

I dreamed I was living in a medieval village of the kind you might find in Europe a few centuries ago. There were cobblestone streets and little Tudor houses. It was a "once upon a time" setting. There was a beautiful castle atop a hill, where the king, with his lords and his ladies, ruled over us peasants in the village. What position did I occupy in the hurry and bustle of our hamlet? How did God show myself to me? I was a child, a small boy. I was the village beggar. I was darkened by dirt, with uncombed and ratted hair. Dressed in rags, I begged in the streets. I was the most inconsequential person in the town. One day, the gates of the castle drew open and the king, with his lords and ladies, who were dressed in elegant clothes and riding beautiful horses, swept down the ramparts, across the drawbridge, and descended the hill into the village. The king, a figure of overwhelming dignity, rode at the front on the whitest horse I have ever seen.

I wanted to see the king up close, but so did everyone else, and I was just the village beggar. In the jostling of the crowd, I pushed myself towards the front and found a place by the side of the road and waited. There were people all around me and I felt very small and unimportant in my rags with my smudged, dirty face and my uncombed hair. Remember, I was the least important individual in the tiny town.

When the king rode by, I knew in my dream consciousness that He was my Savior. He wore a beautiful crown on his head covered with bright gems of every color and hue. As He passed me, He reined his horse to a stop right where I was standing. He looked down at me in compassion and love. I held my hand out because I was the beggar, hoping for something. He took off His crown and He turned it in His hand. His eyes passed over all those bright, beautiful jewels—the reds, the blues, the greens, the yellows—and He chose one for me. It was a bright green gem which He pulled out of its setting in His crown. Then He reached down from His horse and He laid it in my hands. He said, "Lift it up high and let the light catch it. Let it shine out for all the people to see its beauty."

Having done this, He rode on with His accompanying retinue. I looked at my green gem. I turned it over in my hand and saw how truly beautiful His gift was. I held it up like my king had told me. The light caught the gem and shot beautiful rays into every dark corner of the village. The people came running to see its splendors, and in its light I looked like a king. But I knew I was the least important. I was the begging boy of the village.

GIFTS FOR
AND FROM ALL

*W*e are ensured in scripture—by Paul, by the Prophet Joseph Smith, by Moroni—that every man and woman receives a gift from the king. Each one of us who stands in the village as the Savior rides by is offered his or her own gem. He looks at us and removes His crown and He chooses the right gem, the right color and radiance for each individual. "To every man is given a gift by the Spirit of God. To some is given one, and to some is given another, that all may be profited thereby" (D&C 46:11–12). We are to hold our gifts up, that God's light may catch them and shine their goodness into the lives of others, giving hope and love and edification.

Each woman in this Church has a jewel, a gift from her King. If every woman were to hold her gift up high, can you imagine the brilliance and beauty we would all see? What would we see if we could picture all your gems through the lens of the Savior's crown of gifts as we stand by the road receiving what He has chosen for us? Can you visualize that? As all those women lift their hands and let the light catch the reds and blues and greens, a thousand rays of beauty and radiance would blossom out to bring hope to everyone. If we look at one another, we will find hope. We shall know hope in the dawning truth that God is using us to lift and lighten the road others are walking. We *are* His hope, not only the recipients of it. We are creators of it.

In His Hour, in His Time, in His Season

I will conclude with what I perceive to be one of the most infinitely beautiful verses of hope in the scriptures. It is found in the Doctrine and Covenants, section 88. Here Joseph Smith related a parable about the Lord's relationship with all His creations, from multiple worlds to their individual inhabitants. "Unto what shall I liken these kingdoms, that ye may understand?" the Lord instructed. "I will liken these kingdoms unto a man having a field, and he sent forth his servants into the field to dig in the field." Each servant, however, was given a marvelous promise as he departed for his labors. "And he said unto the first: Go ye and labor in the field, and in the first hour I will come

unto you, and ye shall behold the joy of my countenance. And he said unto the second: Go ye also
into the field, and in the second hour I will visit you
with the joy of my countenance. And also unto the
third, saying: I will visit you; and unto the fourth,
and so on unto the twelfth" (D&C 88:46, 51–55).

Since the twelve servants represented all the vast
creations of the Lord (see D&C 88:42–47), the visits would continue into infinity. True to his promise,
the owner began his visits, making each laborer "glad
with the light of the countenance of his lord" (D&C
88:56). We are assured that the lord "tarried with
him all that hour" (D&C 88:56). There is that lovely
word *tarry* used again, as we saw it in the story of the
disciples on the road to Emmaus. I would urge us all
to apply the following wonderful words to ourselves
as we labor in the Lord's field with all His other servants. Let us receive the hope these words generate:
"Thus they all received the light of the countenance
of their lord, *every man in his hour, and in his time, and in
his season . . . ; every man in his own order, until his hour was
finished, . . .* that his lord might be glorified in him,
and he in his lord, that they all might be glorified"

(D&C 88:58, 60; emphasis added). I might also point out that in the parable the Lord does not limit us to just one visit (see v. 59). He returns again and again, bringing with Him the promised joy.

Look to this parable when you need hope. Your visit is coming! Remember the Lord's words, look to them, hold them locked within your hearts: "Each man in his hour, and in his time, and in his season . . . ; every man in his own order, until his hour was finished."

For me that is the hope, the infinite hope: that although it may not be my hour now, nor my time, nor my season, nor my order, yet I know that He *will* come. He is mindful of us, has numbered us, will manifest Himself to us, will remember us, and bless and pray for us. To these peace-engendering words we add one final verb. Yes! He will even *visit* us.

May your time, and your hour, and your season, be soon. May the infinite hope of waiting for those visits fill your life.